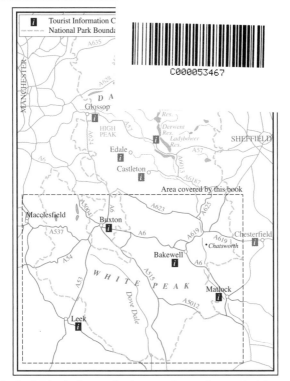

The Peak District is an upland area at the southern end of the Pennine chain; largely within the borders of Derbyshire, but also crossing into Staffordshire, Cheshire, Greater Manchester and Yorkshire. The greater part of the area is contained within the Peak District National Park (founded 1951). Traditionally, the Peak District is divided into two distinct areas: the northern 'Dark Peak' and the southern 'White Peak'. This book covers the southern area.

The distinction between the two areas is geological. The White Peak is based on limestone, creating a landscape of low green hills intersected by narrow valleys. The hills are largely divided into grazing fields by stone walls; the valleys contain typical limestone rock features: caves and low, crumbling cliffs.

The main towns in the area are the spa resort of Buxton (tourist information centre) *(Walk 4)* and Bakewell (national park information centre), on the River Wye *(7,8)*, but there are numerous smaller towns and villages spread throughout the area. The major tourist attractions in the White Peak are the magnificent Chatsworth House – to the east of Bakewell – and the extended gorge of Dovedale. Chatsworth – which is open to the public – is the seat of the Dukes of Devonshire, and is surrounded by splendid woodland and parkland. It is also at the heart of a number of fine footpaths *(8,9,10)*. Dovedale is famous for its extravagant rock formations, which can be easily viewed from the riverside path *(19,20)*.

For those particularly interested in walking through the area's narrow valleys, the other dale walks in the guide are past the old mills in Monsal Dale *(11)*, through the woods of Lathkill Dale *(12)* – plus the connected path along Wolfscote Dale to Monyash *(13)*, and the path which passes the dramatic Thor's Cave – high above the Manifold Valley in a rocky outcrop – before continuing along the wooded dale below *(17,18)*. In addition, there is a walk between Matlock and the riverside resort of Matlock Bath *(14)*. This is not within the national park area, but the sheer cliff of High Tor is one of the most dramatic features in the Peak District.

In the north-east of this area there are two walks along the 'edges' above Curbar and Froggatt *(5,6)*. Edges – long, low cliffs along the top of a slope – are a feature more associated with the Dark Peak, but another – the Roaches – can be seen in the south-west of the area *(23)*. This is an area particularly popular with rock climbers.

Generally speaking, the south-west corner is a little different in character to the rest of the area, tending more towards the type of open moorland found to the north. There is a fine ridge walk above the Goyt Valley *(2)*, as well as a woodland path to a reservoir south of Whaley Bridge *(1)* and a short, steep trail leading to a viewpoint east of Macclesfield *(3)*. Outside the national park area, to the south-west, there are two fine, low-level walks around large reservoirs *(22,24)*.

Taxal & Fernilee Reservoir_____B

walk, through woodland and farmland, up one side of a valley, across dam, and back down the other. Paths generally clear. Length: **miles/6.5km***; Height Climbed:* **360ft/110m** (with undulations).

> reach the start of this walk, drive
mile south of Whaley Bridge on the
5004. There is a long car park on
e west side of the road.

From the middle of the car park a
ear path zig-zags down a wooded
ope. Watch for a gate on the left
d a sign for a footpath. Go through
e gate and follow the clear track
yond.

Follow this track (ignoring the
gned path to the left) to the edge
the trees. Pass through a gate and
ntinue through grazing fields. Stay
ose to the River Goyt, ignoring a
th to the left and a footbridge to the
ght, and continue to the buildings
fore the Fernilee Reservoir dam.

You are now on a tarmac road.
fore the largest building this splits.
ep left, climbing to the end of the
m, then turn right, across the dam.

At the far end of the dam, turn
ght. A clear vehicle track runs
aight as far as Knipe Farm, then
ings left to cross Mill Clough
fore climbing past Madscar Farm.
st above the farm there is a hairpin
nd. Keep left here, following the
d to a junction just before the
ildings at Overton Hall Farm.

Turn right here, onto a clear
ck, and follow it for a little under
nile/1.5km to reach the village of
xal, with its square-towered church.

Turn right immediately before
the church on a metalled path. This
leads to a ford, with a footbridge just
downstream. Cross the bridge and
climb back up to the car park.

2 Shining Tor

A circuit on good paths which climbs, steeply, through woodland to a long moorland ridge providing splendid views. Length: **5½ miles/9km** Height Climbed: **885ft/270m**.

O.S. Sheets 118 & 119 (OL 2

To reach the car park at Errwood Reservoir, drive 4 miles east of Macclesfield on the A537 and turn left onto a minor road. Follow the signs for Goyt Valley at subsequent junctions. When you reach the reservoir, turn right to reach the car park (there are two) at the southern end.

From the car park, follow the path signed for Errwood Hall; passing through a gap in a wall and turning right along the track beyond it. Follow the track into a wooded valley, ignoring paths to right and left. At a sign for Errwood Hall, turn right.

Pass the ruined house and swing left, up another valley. Cross a serpentine footbridge over a stream and continue 20m to reach a junction. Turn right, up steps, to reach a further junction. This time go left (Pym Chair). You pass a further junction (Pym Chair) and a small shrine as you climb up to join the road.

Turn left and climb to the highest point of the road, where there is a sign pointing left for Shining Tor. Follow a clear – often slabbed – path for 2 miles/3km along the ridge to reach the peak of Shining Tor.

At the top, turn left (Cat & Fiddle). Follow a path, with a wall to the right, downhill then up again to reach a junction of walls. Go through a kissing gate in the wall ahead and turn left (Errwood), now with a wall to your left.

At one point a signposted path goes through a gate to the left (this is an alternative return, via Shooter's Clough and Errwood Hall – *see map*) but otherwise stick to the main path return to the car park.

short, steep, varied circuit, passing through farmland and woodland to reach a small reservoir, then climbing to an old quarry and a fine viewpoint. Length: **2¹/₂ miles/4km***; Height Climbed:* **656ft/200m***.*

O.S. Sheet 118 (OL 24)

Tegg's Nose Country Park is just east of Macclesfield – follow the signs for it off the A537. There is an information centre in the car park.

From the edge of the car park overlooking the valley, take the clear track signed as Saddlers Way: a paved track which leads down the slope to join a metalled road. Turn right.

When the road doubles back to the left take the path to the right (there is a sign for the Trail) and continue, with walls to either side. After a short distance you cross a stile by a gate then continue with a wall to your left.

You reach a stream. Cross this by the stepping stones and continue on the clear track beyond, with the stream down to your right at first, and then the reservoir.

Walk down to the end of the reservoir and turn right, along the dam. At the far end there is a small car park and a signpost. Go left (Gritstone Trail), passing through a gate and following a clear, steep path out of the trees and on up the slope to join a clear track which contours around the hill. Turn right.

The track swings left, around the end of Tegg's Nose, and there are fine views: west over Macclesfield and Manchester; south and east into the Peak District. Follow the track past the deep quarry (take care here)

and the interpretive boards providing information about the old gritstone industry.

At a junction, turn right and follow a clear path back to the car park.

4 Buxton Country Park

A circuit through grassland and woodland, passing an old hill-top folly (providing fine views) and the entrance to Poole's Cavern. Length: **2 miles/3km**; *Height Climbed:* **330ft/100m**.

O.S. Sheet 119 (OL 2

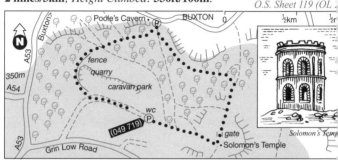

Solomon's Temp

Buxton Country Park comprises a 100 acre/40ha wood on the slope to the south-west of the town, climbing to an area of hummocky grassland covering what was, until the 19th century, a limestone quarry. At the highest point sits a cylindrical folly – Solomon's Temple – with steps up the inside leading to a fine viewpoint. The are numerous paths through the park; the following route passes the main points of interest.

It is possible to walk to the park from the centre of Buxton, but those coming from outside the town should park at the Grin Low car park. To reach this, turn east on the road signed for Grin Low from the A53, on the south-west edge of Buxton, then turn left onto the entrance road to the car park.

Walk on beyond the car park on the path signed for the Temple. At junctions, follow the signs for the

Temple until it becomes visible ahea

Having enjoyed the views from th folly, head straight downhill (ie, hea left at the Temple); passing through gate in a wall and continuing to reac the wood.

Once in the trees head left and follow one of the many small paths down and across the slope. At the bottom of the slope you will find the car park for Poole's Cavern – an extensive limestone cave system which has been one of the great attractions of the Peak District since the 16th century.

From the car park, walk uphill up some steps (signed for Grin Low). A the first junction go straight on (Grin Low); at the next, near the top of the wood, go right (caravan site).

Go through a gate and continue with a fence around a quarry to your left. Follow this fence round to rejo the access road to the car park.

*path along the top of rocky Curbar Edge, with a return through the
—odland below the cliffs. Length:* **3-5 miles/5-8km**; *Height Climbed:*
—0ft/185m.

O.S. Sheet 119 (OL 24)

—e little village of Curbar is 5 miles
—rth of Bakewell by the A619/A623
—d a minor road. Take the minor
—ad east from the village and climb
— to the car park at Curbar Gap.

At the main (paying) car park,
—ere is a path signed for Curbar
—ge. Follow this clear path onto and
—ong the moorland ridge behind the
—ags. The views are terrific.

Continue for a little over a
—ile/1.5km. There are two signpost-
— paths heading down to the left. At
—e second one you have a choice. To
—ntinue along Froggatt Edge, keep
—raight on – it is about a mile/1.5km
—th the public road. To continue with
—e circuit, head half-left on a clear
—th leading to a platform below the
—ne of crags. After about 200 paces a
—th heads left off the platform, down
—to the trees.

Follow this path down to a wall
—ith a gate in it. Turn left along a
—th on the near (upper) side of the
—all. As you approach another wall
—e path splits – keep to the right,
—ading for a green metal gate. Go
—rough this, and a second gate a little
—ay further on, then contour across
—e slope on a clear path, ignoring
—aller paths to right and left.

Houses come into view ahead.
—u reach a wall with a gate in it, and
— sign pointing left for Curbar Gap.
—his last section – through small

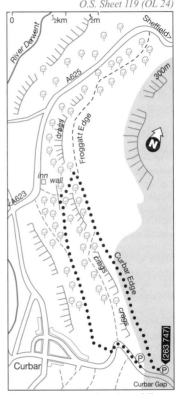

fields on the approach to the public
road – is difficult to describe but easy
to follow. Once on the public road
turn left (being careful to keep out of
the way of traffic) and climb back up
to the car park.

6 Baslow Edge

*A climb onto rocky Baslow Edge, and a return through the grazing land and farmland below the rocks. Length: **4 miles/6.5km**; Height Climbed **950ft/290m**. Possible link with Walk 5.*

O.S. Sheet 119 (OL ..

Start this walk from the car park in the village of Baslow, 4 miles east of Bakewell on the A619. Walk out of the car park entrance, cross (carefully) the two roads directly ahead then continue up the road called Eaton Hill. When the road swings to the left go right, up Bar Road.

The road leaves the houses and continues to climb, eventually reaching a gate leading onto the moorland.

Beyond the gate the road becomes an unmetalled track. It levels out and splits. A detour to the right here leads to Wellington's Monument. Otherwise, keep to the left, passing the striking Eagle Stone and running on through moorland behind the top of the Baslow Edge crags (a detour to the left will lead to the crags).

The path ends at the public road. If you wish to continue along Walk 5, cross the road. To complete this shorter walk, turn left along a rough footpath above the road. After a short distance you reach a sign for a footpath, pointing left through a gate.

The rough path goes downhill through a jumble of old walls, then passes through a gap in a wall to reach a four-way junction of paths. Go left, to reach a gate marked by an Access Land sign. Beyond this, follow a clear, rough path (ignoring paths to right and left) through rough grazing land below the crags.

Pass a signposted four-way junction (go straight on) and cross a wall just beyond. Continue, with a wall now to your right. You quickly join a track between walls. Follow this until it turns right, through the wall. At this point keep straight on along a clear path.

The path starts with a wall to the right; beyond a gate/stile it continues above a slope with a wall to the left. Beyond the next gate, cross one more small field to rejoin Bar Road.

complex circuit on rough paths and quiet public roads, through
rmland and woodland. Steep in places. Length: **2¹/2-5 miles/4-8km;**
eight Climbed: **560ft/170m.**

O.S. Sheet 119 (OL 24)

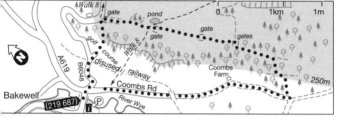

art this route as for Walk 8, climb-
g to the metalled road at the top of
e wood. For this walk, turn right
the sign for the footpath, passing
rough a gate and continuing along a
ne between walls.

When the lane ends, continue on
clear track heading towards a stand
conifers on the horizon. As you
proach the trees the track splits.
o right, along the edge of the trees.
fter a short distance the track splits.
o right (yellow arrow), on a very
int path heading towards the right-
nd edge of a pond.

There are two gates in the fence
hich extends to the right of the
nd. Aim for the larger, right-hand,
te. (NB: it is possible to make a
orter loop from this point – *see*
alk 8.)

Beyond the gate you are in a large
eld, sloping from right to left, with
es at the top of the slope. A faint
ack leads up and across the slope
a gate/stile in a fence. Go through
is gate and continue in the same di-

rection, aiming for the left-hand edge
of a block of trees jutting out from the
wood to the right.

Walk 100m along the edge of
the trees and go through a gate to
the right and another just beyond it.
Continue beyond these on a clear path
through the conifers. Initially there is
a fallen down wall to the right of the
path. When the wall ends the path
swings to the left: running along an
open ride for a short distance before
edging into the trees to the right. The
path (badly rutted on this section)
runs to the right of a wall for a short
way then peels away, down the slope
to reach a signposted junction.

Go left at the junction (bridleway).
After a short distance the track forks.
Keep right, edging down and across
the slope to reach a complicated junction on the edge of the wood.

Go hard right at the junction and
follow a clear track down a pleasant, farmed valley. Pass the ruined
Coombs Farm and continue down
Coombs Road, back to Blackwell.

8 Bakewell to Chatsworth

*A complex loop, through farmland and woodland, linking Bakewell and
the village of Edensor, with a possible extension to Chatsworth House.*
Length: 5-6 miles/8-9.5km; Height Climbed: 590ft/180m.

O.S. Sheet 119 (OL

Park in Bakewell and find Bridge
St (A619). Follow the road across
the bridge over the River Wye and
keep right at the junction just beyond
(Station Rd/B6048). Ignore Coombs
Rd, which cuts off to the right almost
immediately, and follow the road as it
climbs up the edge of the village.

The road forks (there is a small
post box to the right at this point).
Go right. The road crosses a bridge
over the old railway line. Just
beyond, opposite a white house, a
clear bridleway heads off to the right
(Chatsworth).

A track crosses almost immediately. Ignore this and continue straight

uphill to reach the edge of the golf
course. Ring the bell (as instructed)
and cross the course. On the far side
continue straight uphill through the
wood, ignoring paths to right and left
to reach a metalled minor road on the
top edge of the wood.

Go right, uphill, along the road.
Immediately, a footpath starts to the
right (*see* Walk 7). Ignore this and
continue along the road for half a
mile/1km: climbing over a low hill
then dropping to reach a fork, with
a very clear, rough track heading off
ahead-right. Keep right, down the
track. As the track descends you see
your first view of Chatsworth, behin

steeple of the church in Edensor. The track joins a metalled road and ntinues down into the village. As u walk through the village, with its aint and picturesque architecture, tch for a sign to the right, at the ot of a set of steps, for a footpath to wsley.

At this point you have a choice. **you wish to continue to Chats-orth**, keep straight on to the foot of e village, cross the road, and follow e clear path through parkland yond. There and back, this will add nile/1.5km to the total length of the lk. **To continue with the circuit** n right at the sign and climb to a tal gate in a wall with an area of rkland beyond.

At this point you lose the path for vhile. Looking ahead-right from e wall you should see a post with ellow arrow on it. Walk up to e post and continue in the direc-n indicated, passing to the left of a nd of trees and continuing to climb til the rest of the parkland becomes ible.

Looking ahead you will see a mp of conifers ahead and to the ht, with another, longer conifer od, with a wooden fence around to the left. Aim for the right-hand ge of the wooden fence.

Beyond the fence, continue in the ne direction, climbing towards the od at the top of the hill. Before u reach it, you pass to the right of mall plantation and a yellow arrow nts towards a gate on the edge of wood.

Beyond the gate/stile a clear track runs through the trees. Follow this through the narrow wood to another gate at the far side. Beyond this there is a rough sheep path across a field. Follow this for a short distance to reach a signposted junction. Go right here, turning off the path onto an old, grassed-over track.

A conifer wood starts to the left. Level with the far end of it you pass through a gate in a fence. Aim for the top left-hand corner of the field beyond – it is not visible, but you can work out where it is.

At the corner of the field there is a pond. Just before the pond, go through a gate to the left, then skirt around the edge of the water to reach another gate in a fence, beyond which there is a signposted junction.

Head off ahead-left (Bakewell), passing to the left of a small stand of trees and then continuing, aiming for the lowest part of the field, down to the left.

As you approach the lowest point you will see a gate in the fence to the left and a sign for a footpath. Go through the gate and follow a rough path down through a wood, ignoring clearer paths to right and left.

At the foot of the wood, ring the bell, cross the golf course, and follow a path between fences to a bridge over the old railway. Beyond that, go through a gate/stile into a field and walk down the left-hand side of the field to reach Coombs Road. Turn right along the road to return to the start.

Two loops centred on Chatsworth House – seat of the Dukes of Devonshire – which can be combined to make one walk. The paths pass through parkland and woodland. **9)** *Length:* **3½ miles/5.5km**; *Height Climbed:* **340ft/115m**. **10)** *Length:* **5 miles/8km**; *Height Climbed:* **490ft/150m**. *Length (combined walk):* **7½ miles/12km**. *Possible link with Walks 6 and 8.*

O.S. Sheet 119 (OL

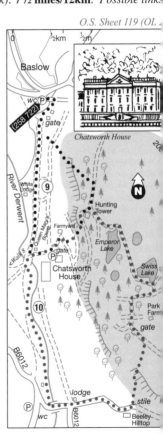

Walk 9) Start this walk from the car park in the village of Baslow, 4 miles east of Bakewell on the A619. (NB: If this car park is full there is another at Chatsworth House.)

Leave the car park by the entrance and turn right along the road, quickly crossing a bridge over a stream. Beyond, turn first right at a signposted junction (Chatsworth). Walk past houses (ignore a footbridge to the right) to reach a large gate.

Immediately beyond the gate a signpost marks a concessionary path to Stand Tower. This is the return route, but for now keep straight on: ignoring tracks to right and left and continuing through the parkland, with the river down to the right, to reach the bridge in front of the majestic Chatsworth House.

If you are linking this walk with Walk 10, turn right, across the bridge. **To complete Walk 9** turn left, towards the house. The house is open to the public (there is also a shop and a restaurant), but for this route keep left to enter the car park.

Walk to the top of the car park. A notice board shows the way to the 'farmyard'. Follow the metalled road indicated, passing through a ate. Ignore the road to the right just beyond and continue. Just beyond the entrance to the farmyard there is a hairpin bend. When you come level with buildings to your right you will see a small path staring to the left. This climbs steeply, on stone steps beside a stream, to reach a metalled road. The dramatic Hunting Tower (16th century) is directly ahead of you (private).

Turn left along the metalled road. Just beyond the tower you reach a junction. Go left here (Robin Hood). After half a mile/1km turn left at a sign for Baslow.

Follow a rough path down and cross the slope through conifers. At the bottom of the wood you re-enter the park. Aim half-right down the slope on a track. At subsequent junctions continue in roughly the same direction to rejoin the original path – there is no clear route, just avoid going too far to the right.

Walk 10 This walk is described from the Chatsworth car park, but it can also be started from the car park by the bridge (*see* map).

From the car park, walk down to the bridge in front of Chatsworth House and cross the River Derwent. At the far side turn left immediately and follow the river through parkland for a little over a mile/1.5km to reach the public road by an old, narrow bridge.

Turn left, over the bridge (be wary of traffic here and until you turn off the main road) and continue by the road until it turns to the right. At this point a driveway (with a gatehouse) and a narrow public road head off to the left. Take the public road.

The road climbs steeply uphill to a farm (Beeley Hilltop) then continues as a track. Just beyond the farm there is a sign for a footpath to the left. Cross a stile into a field. Cross the corner of the field to reach a gate/stile.

Beyond this a clear, rough path heads left, up and across a bracken-covered slope, to join a track at the top of the slope. Turn left along this to reach a gate/stile at the edge of a wood.

Continue on a clear track through the wood. A track/path comes in from the left. Ignore this and continue on the main track, swinging right then left to reach a signposted four-way junction. Keep straight on (Robin Hood).

Continue on the main track, through farmland and woodland; passing to the left of Swiss Lake then to the right of Emperor Lake. Ignore tracks to the left beyond this and continue to Hunting Tower (16th century). The track passes to the right of the tower to reach a signposted junction. A turn to the right here (Robin Hood) links with Walk 9. To complete Walk 10, keep straight on; the track continuing to curve to the left and becoming metalled.

When you are level with the tower again, a path starts to the right. Follow this downhill, on stone steps, to reach a metalled road. Turn right along this to return to the start.

A circuit starting up a narrow dale, passing old mills and railway architecture, then returning through farmland. Paths generally good, but steep in places. Length: **6¹/₂ miles/10.5km***; Total Height Climbed (there are severe undulations):* **1,100ft/330m.**

O.S. Sheet 119 (OL 2

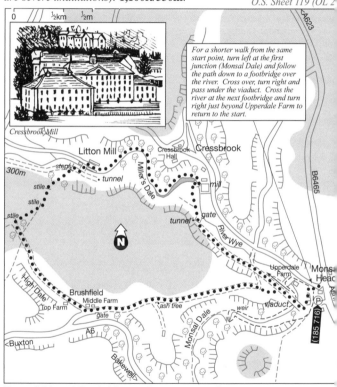

For a shorter walk from the same start point, turn left at the first junction (Monsal Dale) and follow the path down to a footbridge over the river. Cross over, turn right and pass under the viaduct. Cross the river at the next footbridge and turn right just beyond Upperdale Farm to return to the start.

To reach Monsal Head, drive a mile west from Bakewell on the A6, turn right onto the A6020 then, almost immediately, left onto the B6465. Monsal Head, on the lip of Monsal

Dale, is 1¹/₂ miles along this road.

Park in the long stay car park (pay) and walk past the hotel to reach a minor public road. Turn left for a short distance. When the road bends ight there is a gap in a wall ahead nd a signposted junction. Go right (Monsal Viaduct) and zig-zag down he slope to the old railway viaduct.

Cross the viaduct and continue long the line of the old railway ignoring paths cutting off to left and ight) for a mile/1.5km to reach the losed-off entrance to a tunnel.

Go through a gate to the right, just efore the tunnel, and continue along rough path which contours across he slope, noting the view ahead of he fine Cressbrook Mill. A faint path limbs away to the left. Ignore this nd continue on the main path, which ow begins to descend.

The path joins the River Wye by pool behind a weir, with cliffs op-osite. Cut back to the right to join footbridge. Cross over (the mill uildings are down to your right) and urn left onto the concessionary path vhich runs along the foot of the cliffs NB: if this path is flooded, look for he alternative path above the cliffs).

Follow this clear path by the river, hrough a dramatic, winding gorge, until you reach the end of the public oad at Litton Mill. Walk along the village street until a sign points left or Monsal Trail. Turn left here, cross footbridge over the river then climb o rejoin the old railway.

Turn right. Almost immediately here are steps to the left, leading onto disused bridge. At the top of the teps turn left (Priestcliffe), crossing stile and following a rough path up nd across the slope to reach the top ight-hand corner of a grazing field.

Cross a stile by a gate (yellow ar-

row) and continue uphill with a fence to your right. After a short distance, cross a stile to the right to enter a nar-row field. Walk up the left-hand side of this field. At the far end, cross a stile to join a clear track.

Turn left along the track and follow it until it reaches the end of a metalled road, just as you approach Brushfield. Pass a farm and then the end of the holiday cottages at Middle Farm to reach a signposted junction. Turn left here (Monsal Dale) and walk along the front of the buildings.

At the end of the buildings there is a wooden gate. Go through this and continue along a metalled driveway. You reach a metal gate and beyond this the track, no longer metalled, continues, with a wooded slope down to the right and a wall running paral-lel, off to the left.

When the trees end to the right, go through another gate and follow the track across a field to an ash tree with field entrances to either side. Go through the left-hand entrance (Mon-sal Dale) and continue, now with a wall to the right.

After a further gate/stile, continue with the wall to your right. Next you encounter twin gates. Follow the track through the right-hand (wooden) gate and continue, now running above a slope down to the right.

The track begins to drop down a ridge, with Monsal Head visible ahead. When the track swings hard left, a bridleway continues straight on. Follow this down to the old railway line and turn right, over the viaduct, to return to the start.

Walks South Peak District

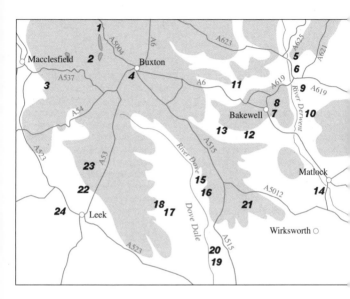

Grades

A ...... Full walking equipment required

B ...... Strong walking footwear and waterproof clothing required

C ...... Comfortable walking footwear recommended

[B/C, etc ...... Split grades refer either to multiple route titles or to the fact that the single route described can be walked either in its entirety or in shorter, less gruelling sections.]

— www.pocketwalks.com —

Published by: Hallewell Publications, The Milton,
Foss, Pitlochry, Perthshire PH16 5NQ
Printed by: J. Thomson Printers, Glasgow

	walk	grade
1	Taxal & Fernilee Reservoir	B
2	Shining Tor	A
3	Tegg's Nose Trail	B
4	Buxton Country Park	C
5	Curbar Edge	B
6	Baslow Edge	B
7	Bakewell Loop	B/C
8	Bakewell & Chatsworth	B
9	Baslow & Chatsworth	C
10	Chatsworth Loop	B
11	Monsal Head	B
12	Lathkill Dale	B/C
13	Monyash Loop	B
14	Matlock Bath & Matlock	B
15	Hartington & Pilsbury	B
16	Hartington & Wolfscote Dale	B
17	Thor's Cave	C
18	Thor's Cave & Wetton Hill	B
19	Thorpe Cloud	B
20	Dovedale & Mill Dale	B
21	Roystone Grange Trail	B
22	Tittesworth Reservoir	B
23	The Roaches	A/B
24	Rudyard Reservoir	B

A lineal walk along the narrow, wooded, limestone dale, passing relics of the old lead mining industry. Length: up to **4 miles/6.5km** *(includin return); Height Climbed:* **395ft/120m**. *Possible link with Walk 13. Par may be closed at times in the winter.*

O.S. Sheet 119 (OL 2

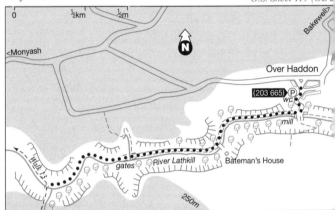

Start this walk from the village of Over Haddon. To reach it, drive a mile south-west from Bakewell on the B5055 then turn left onto the minor road to Over Haddon. Once in the village, follow the signs for the car park.

A road runs parallel to the car park. Follow this down the steep slope into the dale (NB: there is a small car park for the disabled near the foot of the slope). The road ends at the River Lathkill, where there is a cottage, a footbridge over the river and a ruined mill. Turn right here, following a clear track up the near side of the river (NB: this section is along a permitted footpath and may be closed for some days during the winter).

The track runs for a little over a mile/1.5km through mixed woodlan passing caves and mines along the way (a footbridge leads across the river to the ruin of Bateman's House where a steel ladder leads to the entrance to one of the shafts). At the end of this section you reach a gate in a wall.

To continue up the dale, pass through this gate and another just beyond. The path is rougher beyon this point; the dale still deep but less wooded. After a little over a mile/1.5km you join Walk 13. From here it is possible to continue up to the village of Monyash (a total distance of 7 miles/11km), but for th walk return by the same route.

circuit on rough paths, starting through farmland and returning
rough the dramatic scenery of upper Lathkill Dale. Length: 4¹/2
iles/7km; *Height Climbed:* **330ft/100m**. *Possible link with Walk 12.*

O.S. Sheet 119 (OL 24)

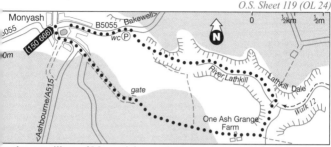

e pleasant village of Monyash is
¹2 miles west of Bakewell on the
5055. Park either in the village or at
e car park just to the east.

From the centre of the village, turn
to the road for Ashbourne. The
ad swings left, past a pond, then
ht. At that point keep straight on
gn: Limestone Way) on a smaller
ad. When this second road swings
ht keep straight on again, this time
a clear track with walls to either
e.

The lane ends at a gate/stile.
ntinue beyond on a clear path with
vall to the right. After 60m there is
tone stile over the wall. Cross this
d cut across the corner of the field
yond, aiming for a gate and a post.

Cross a stile here and continue
h a wall to the left through two
lds. Near the end of the second
re is a stone stile to the left. Cross
s and continue with the wall now
your right. At the end of a long
field there is a gate to the right. Go
through this and follow the clear track
down to One Ash Grange Farm.

Once amongst the buildings,
ignore the path to Cales Farm to the
right and continue to a fork. Keep left
here. At the next fork go right, dropping to pass between a metal barn and
some old stone barns. At the end of
the buildings, climb down a few steep
steps then walk down the low part of
the long field ahead.

Go through a wooden gate and
descend between rocky outcrops. The
path is rocky and steep for a section
before reaching the bottom of the
wooded dale. Turn left, down the
near side of the dale.

When this dale joins Lathkill Dale,
cross a footbridge over the River
Lathkill and turn left. A clear path
runs up the dramatic dale (stick to
the path to avoid old mine shafts).
Continue beyond the head of the dale,
through fields, to return to the road.

A complex circuit linking the two towns, following the wooded slopes and dramatic cliffs to either side of the River Derwent. Paths steep in places. Terrific views. Length: **5 miles/8km**; *Total Height Climbed:* **820ft/250m.**

O.S. Sheet 119 (OL 2

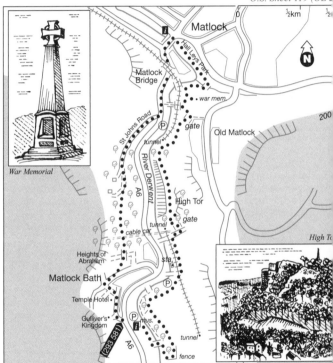

War Memorial

The little riverside resort of Matlock Bath – first developed as a spa town in the 1800s – is 2 miles south of Matlock on the A6. The two towns are linked by the high-sided gorge of the River Derwent, dominated by the

peaked cliff of High Tor. This walk can be started from either end, but is described from Matlock Bath.

Walk to the south end of the town to find the large pink building housing the Mining Museum and TIC. Walk a short distance down the main road then turn first right (Gulliver's Kingdom).

The road doubles back up and across the slope. Ignore a road cutting off to the left and continue past the Temple Hotel. A little beyond, turn left up West Bank. You quickly reach a junction with Orchard Road. Go straight on at this point, climbing a footpath to join another road.

Turn right, along the road. After a very short distance a footpath starts on the left (Matlock). The path starts climbing through woodland – eventually crossing a wooden footbridge over a driveway then passing under the line of the cable cars – before descending to join a farm access road.

Turn right down the access road. This leads you to a metalled public road. Turn right down this to rejoin the A6.

Turn left along the A6 and follow it through Matlock Bridge to reach the road bridge over the river. Cross this and turn first right beyond.

You are now in Hall Leys Park. Walk straight on until you see a sign pointing right for Pic Tor. Cross a bridge over a mill stream and turn right just beyond, on a path through the parkland by the river.

Watch for a sign for the war memorial and turn left at this point. Climb to a junction. Turn left to visit the memorial, then return to the junction and continue in the original direction. This path drops to join a metalled path.

Turn left up the metalled path. At a junction on the edge of some houses turn back-right, through the entrance to High Tor Grounds. Continue climbing on a clear path until you reach the top of High Tor (take great care anywhere near the edge). The views from here are spectacular.

The path continues beyond, winding down to exit the grounds through a handsome gate (the cable car station is just to the right at this point). Beyond the gate, turn right down a metalled track.

Just before the track passes under the railway line there is a sign pointing left for Lovers Walk. Go left here, following a metalled track beside the railway. Just after passing the Swiss-style station buildings, cross the railway (take care here: stop, look, listen).

At the next gate go half-left (Lovers Walk). Walk diagonally across the car park to reach the start of a gravel path, climbing up and across the slope. There are a number of paths through the woods above the river here. For the longest walk, keep left at all the junctions in the wood. This will lead you past a good viewpoint and on to a rough path running along the edge of the trees with a fence to the left.

When a fence bars your way forward, turn right and start descending the slope on a flight of old stone steps. The path eventually doubles back to join the riverside path.

Turn right along the river path to reach a footbridge. Cross this to return to Matlock Bath.

15 Hartington & Pilsbury

A walk out along a quiet public road to the site of a Norman keep, and a return through pleasant farmland. Fine views. Length: **6¹/₂ miles/ 10.5km***; Height Climbed:* **230ft/70m***.*

O.S. Sheet 119 (OL 2

The village of Hartington is 11 miles south of Buxton on the A515/B5054. Park in the car park, walk into the centre of the village and turn left onto the road signed for Pilsbury.

Follow this quiet road through farmland for 2 miles/3km to reach the hamlet of Pilsbury. Beyond the houses, the road doubles back, up to the right. Continue until, just before a barn, there is a signposted junction.

To visit Pilsbury Castle, turn left (Crowdicote), through a gate. Head half-left from the gate; crossing a field to reach a stone stile over a wall. 20m beyond you go through a gap in a wall, then continue with a wall to the right to reach a point overlooking the grassy mounds where the castle once stood. Return to the road.

To complete the circuit, turn right (Hartington). Cross a stile over a fence and head half-left to reach a gap in a wall with a post at it. Beyond this, you continue up the lowest part of the grazing land ahead.

When you reach a transverse wall turn right (Hartington) and climb to a junction with another wall. Cross the wall ahead and continue, level now, with the wall running off to the left.

Follow a faint path past two field corners and on to a gate in a wall. Cross the next field to reach a gap in a wall. Head half-right from this to reach a further gate.

The path is clearer now. Go straight on, over three further walls, to enter a rougher grazing area where the route is marked by posts. When a wall comes in from the left, continue with the wall to your left and a slope down to the right.

Join a driveway on a hairpin bend and turn left. At a field gate turn right for a short way to reach a small gate. Go through this and turn right, with a wall to your right. After 90m cross a stile to your right and then follow the yellow arrows through fields to join the public road to the left of a barn.

Turn right to return to Hartington.

low level circuit through farmland and along two fine, narrow dales.
:ngth: **6 miles/9.5km**; _Height Climbed:_ **330ft/100m**.

O.S. Sheet 119 (OL 24)

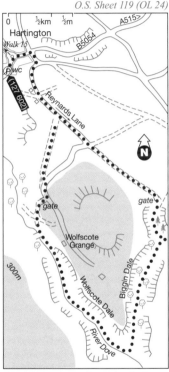

e picturesque village of Hartington
11 miles south of Buxton on the
515/B5054. Park in the car park.
om the centre of the village, walk
st (the Ashbourne road) then turn
st right up Hall Bank.

After a short climb you reach
unction. Turn right (Wolfscote
ange Farm) and continue climbing,
t of the village.

Follow this narrow road (Reynards
ne), ignoring tracks to right and
t, for ³/₄ mile/1km, until it cuts hard
ght at a junction. At this point go
aight on along a rough track. After
ew yards this splits. Go right (Big-
n Dale).

Follow this track until it ends at
gate. Beyond this, continue on the
th down into Biggin Dale. Swing
ght, down the grassy bottom of the
le, with a wood to your left. When
e wood ends turn left, into a smaller
le. Go through a gate to reach a
gnpost, then turn right (Wolfscote
ale) and continue down Biggin
ale, with a wall to your right at first.

Follow the clear, rough path down
e pleasant dale for a mile/1.5km
reach the River Dove. Turn right
re, following a clear path up narrow
olfscote Dale for 1¹/₂ miles/2.5km
reach a footbridge over the river at
e head of the dale.

Do not cross the bridge. Turn
ght instead, following a clear track
tween walls, up and across the

slope. Ignore a track coming in from
the right and follow the track up to a
gate leading onto the public road.

Turn left along the road. After
it bends hard right take the second
signposted path to the left and follow
a clear track back to Reynards lane.

Turn left to return to the start.

17) *A short walk through farmland from Wetton to the dramatic Thor's Cave and back. Length:* **2 miles/3km**; *Height Climbed:* **295ft/90m**. **18** *A longer circuit passing the cave then continuing by the River Manifold and returning by Wetton Hill. Length:* **4-6 miles/6.5-9.5km**; *Height Climbed:* up to **490ft/150m**. *Paths generally clear, but some navigation needed on return.*

O.S. Sheet 119 (OL.

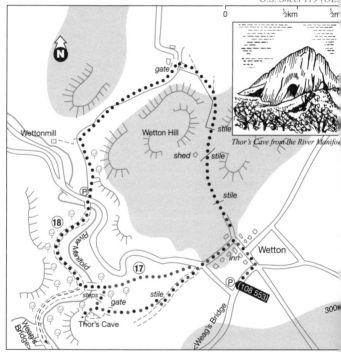

Thor's Cave from the River Manifol

There are three possible car parks for **Walk 18**. The walk is described from the village of Wetton (9 miles north-west of Ashbourne on minor roads), but there is also parking at Wettonmill and Weag's Bridge (*see* map – add 2 miles/3km if starting from the latter, and start the walk along the metalled track by the river, which gives fine views of the hill of Thor's Cave).

Walk 17 should be started from
[We]tton.

Walks 17 & 18) From the car park
[at] Wetton, walk back into the centre
[of] the village and turn onto the road
[sig]ned for Wettonmill. Follow this to
[a] junction at the edge of the village.
[Go] straight on here. A short distance
[bey]ond, turn left onto a clear track
[(Th]or's Cave).

[After] a little over half a mile/1km
[the]re is a stile over the wall to the
[rig]ht. Cross this and continue with
[the] wall to your left. The path
[bec]omes clearer and reaches a small
[gate], just before you reach the rock
[into] which the cave is set. Keep right
[bey]ond the gate and follow the path
[rou]nd to the entrance of the cave.

[Great care must be taken when ex-
[plo]ring the cave. The main entrance,
[30f]t/10m high, is set into the bare
[roc]k high above the river below and
[the] rocks around the entrance can be
[slip]py when damp.

[Having explored the cave, retrace
[yo]ur steps but veer left down the path/
[ste]ps leading down through the wood
[int]o the valley. The path reaches a
[sig]nposted junction.

Walk 17) Turn right, up the little
[wo]oded valley, to reach a gate leading
[int]o a field. Continue up through two
[fiel]ds. At the top corner of the second
[fiel]d a gap leads onto the road on the
[edg]e of the village.

Walk 18) Turn left (Manifold
[Valle]y), quickly reaching a footbridge
[ove]r the River Manifold.

[Cross the bridge and turn right,
[fol]lowing a metalled track until it

crosses a bridge over the river and
joins the public road. Head half-right,
across the road, and pass through a
small parking area to reach a gate/stile
leading into a field.

From the gate, head half-left along
a grassy track, with a steep slope
rising to the right and a wall off to the
left. The track dog-legs to the right
(ignore a path to the left at this point)
and continues with the ground rising
steeply to either side.

Continue in this direction for half
a mile/1km to reach a gate at the end
of a public road. There is a house
to the left, just beyond, and opposite
that a sign for a footpath (Wetton).
Turn right here: go through a gap in a
wall, drop to cross a slab bridge over
a stream, then climb a grassy path
which runs parallel to a wall off to
the right.

Follow the wall as it edges round
to the right. Just short of the water-
shed a fence crosses the way. Cross
the stile over this and head half-left,
diagonally across a field. Your objec-
tive is not visible at first, but midway
across the field a stile over a fence
becomes visible.

Beyond the stile a clear path leads
up and across the slope. This leads to
a stone stile over a wall. Cross this
and continue, with a wall to the right
and an old quarry ahead-right. The
route is difficult to describe at this
point – there are a number of junctions – but easy to understand on the
ground: just keep straight on to join
the end of the public road. Follow
this downhill to return to Wetton.

19) *A short, steep climb to the fine viewpoint of Thorpe Cloud. Length* **2 miles/3km** *(including return); Height Climbed:* **475ft/145m**. **20)** *A lineal walk up the most celebrated of the Peak District dales, passing numerous fine limestone features, plus a loop through farmland at the north end of the dale. Length:* **7 miles/11km**; *Height Climbed:* **460ft/140m**.

O.S. Sheet 119 (OL

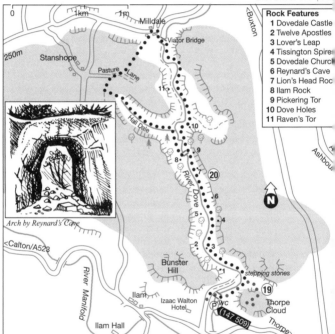

Rock Features
1. Dovedale Castle
2. Twelve Apostles
3. Lover's Leap
4. Tissington Spire
5. Dovedale Church
6. Reynard's Cave
7. Lion's Head Roc
8. Ilam Rock
9. Pickering Tor
10. Dove Holes
11. Raven's Tor

Arch by Reynard's Cave

Walks 19 & 20) The village of Thorpe is 3 miles/5km north of Ashbourne along minor roads. From there, Dovedale is clearly signed. Turn up the minor road to the car park (fee), which sits at the mouth of the

dale below the twin peaks of Thorpe Cloud (to the right) and Bunster Hil (to the left).

From the car park, start walking up the dale on a clear road. Quite quickly you reach a split, with a

dge crossing the River Dove to the
ht. The left-hand track leads to the
pping stones over the river, further
   If the water is low, you can risk
s; otherwise, cross the bridge and
n left on a rough path up the far
e of the river.

As you reach the stepping stones a
h heads off to the right.

Walk 19) To climb Thorpe Cloud,
n right here. The clear, rough,
ep path climbs to the left of a ridge
fore joining the top of the ridge
 following it to the top of the hill.
m the top there is a fine view of
orpe, Ilam Hall (youth hostel),
nster Hill and the hills to the north.
Descend by the same path.

Walk 20) To continue up
vedale, keep straight on at the
ction, following the clear path by
 side of the river.

There is a succession of dramatic
logical features to be seen as you
nb the dale (*see* map), starting with
vedale Castle on the far side of the
er. The path then climbs steps to
ch Lovers Leap before dropping
k down to the river.

Beyond the impressive stone arch
front of Reynard's Cave the dale
rows before passing a footbridge
r the river by the sloping Ilam
ck. Keep to the right of the river
 the moment and continue (ignor-
 the path to the right for Alsop en
Dale beyond the caves of Dove
les) to reach Viator Bridge at the
e village of Milldale.

It is possible to return by the
ne route, but if you wish to extend

the walk then cross the bridge and
turn left along the public road, just
beyond. After a short distance you
will see a sign for a footpath to the
left, pointing up to the left of a stone
cottage.

Follow the rough, steep path, with
a wall to the left, up a narrow, short
valley. At the top there is a transverse
wall with a gate in it. Go through this
and cross the field ahead to reach a
narrow gap in the wall opposite (NB:
not the gate to the left, which leads
into a different field). Walk along the
bottom of the next two fields with a
wall to your left.

Beyond the end of the second field
you continue with the wall now to
your right. This leads to a gap leading onto a lane. Turn right along this
for 80m to reach a pedestrian gate to
the left.

Head off to the right across the
field beyond to reach a small gate.
Beyond this you are in an L-shaped
field. Walk straight on, quickly joining a wall to your right and continuing to another transverse wall.

This time, do not cross the wall but
instead turn left down its near side,
heading towards the top of Hall Dale.
Cross a stile over a transverse wall
and continue across the bottom of a
narrow field, with a wall to you right,
to reach a wooden gate.

Follow the rough path down the
dale to reach a junction by the River
Dove. Turn right here to return to the
footbridge by Ilam Rock.

Cross the bridge and turn right to
return to the start.

21 **Royestone Grange Trail**

A low-level circuit through farmland, passing places of ancient – and more modern – archaeological interest. Mostly on good tracks, but muddy in places. Length: **4 miles/6.5km**; *Height Climbed:* undulating.

O.S. Sheet 119 (OL 2

This walk starts from the Minninglow car park. To reach this, turn south (for Parwich) off the A5012 at Pikehall (17 miles south-east of Buxton on the A515/A5012). Follow this for a mile, until you pass under an old railway line, then turn left to reach the car park.

Walk out of the far end of the car park, cross a metalled road and continue along the line of the old railway; swinging right, crossing a dramatic stone embankment then passing through a cutting.

Beyond the far end of the cutting there is a junction. Go ahead-left (yellow arrow), crossing a stile to enter a rutted lane. This runs level for a short distance then begins to climb, at which point there is a sign for the Trail to the right. Cross a stone stile then walk down the field beyond to reach an arch under the railway.

Walk down the low part of the field beyond the arch to reach a gap in a wall where a gate used to be. Go through this and continue with a wall to your left. Shortly before the end of the field there is a stile to the left. Cross this and carry on with the wall to your right, passing the buildings of Roystone Grange Farm.

Continue until you reach a wicket gate with a yellow arrow on it to your right. Go through this and then diagonally across the field beyond to

reach a stone stile over a wall.

You are now on a metalled track. A short detour to the left leads to a handsome 19th-century pump house near the site of a medieval farm. Having visited these, walk back up the track, passing the farm (and the site a Roman farm beyond) and continue uphill to reach Minninglow Lane.

Turn left here and continue to reach a road junction. Turn right to return to the start.

*waymarked circuit, on good paths, around a reservoir, passing through
~~~odland and farmland. Length:* **5 miles/8km**; *Height Climbed:* undu-
~~~ing. Visitor centre, restaurant and shop at car park.*

O.S. Sheet 118 (OL24)

reach the start of this walk, drive
miles north-east from Leek on the
~3 then turn left onto the minor road
~ Meerbrook. Turn left after a mile,
~the sign for the reservoir.

At the back of the car park there
~ a sign for Woodland Walks. Start
~~ng a very clear path, with a play
~a to the left. There are some
~ctions in the woods near the start:
~low the yellow arrows. If yellow
~ows point two ways, keep right.
The path – initially suitable for
~eelchairs – becomes rougher and
~re undulating as it winds around a
~ies of bays to reach the end of the
~ervoir, but there is no real doubt
~ut the route. Go through a gate to
~ onto the dam.

At the far end of the dam, climb a
~ht of steps and veer right along a
~ck. This becomes a footpath and
~nbs to a wooden gate. Just beyond
~ you join a metalled track.
Go right here (sign for Long Walk)
~ follow the driveway through
~th Hillswood Farm. At the
~nposted junction just beyond keep
~ight on (Meerbrook) to reach a
~ction with the public road.
Turn right along the road (narrow,
~e careful of traffic) and continue
~il a track opens up to the right
~vern & Trent Water). Follow this
~ck to the reservoir and turn left.

Follow the path by the water up
to the road. Turn right, crossing the
reservoir, then turn right again at the
car park entrance to return to the start.

A rough path along a line of crags much used by climbers. Possible return on a quiet public road or extension to a dramatic chasm. Lengt 3¹/₂-6¹/₄ miles/5.5-10.5km; Height Climbed: 575ft/175m (main route) 390ft/120m (on extension).

O.S. Sheets 118 & 119 (OL

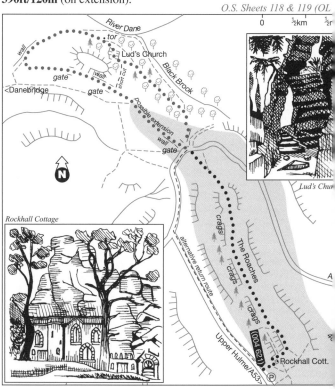

The Roaches is a dramatic line of crags, beloved of rock climbers. To reach it, drive 8 miles south of Buxton on the A53 and turn into Upper Hulme. The road west from

the village leads along the bottom c the crags.

Park in the long car park which runs beside the road and look for a bus stop. Go through a break in the

...ll here and follow a clear track
... the slope. When this main track
...ads right, take a clear path to the
..., climbing to the wall along the
...nt of the eccentric Rockhall Cot-
...e (private).

...Turn left along the wall. After a
...ort distance go right, through a gap
...he wall, and walk straight uphill,
...ough trees, with a wall to your
...ht. This leads to the foot of a flight
...steep stone steps.

...Climb the steps. At the top, keep
...ight on along a faint sheep path;
...sing to the right of the higher crags
...oin a clear, rough footpath which
...s along behind them.

...Turn left along this path, which
...ings left, climbs to the edge of the
...gs then runs along the ridge behind
...m. Follow this clear path for $1^{1}/_{2}$
...es – making occasional forays to
...ir left to peer over the crags – to
...ch the minor public road which
...s around the end of the hill.

...At this point you have a choice.
...u can return by the same route
...you can turn left and follow the
...et public road back to the start
...is route offers fine views from the
...t of the crags). Alternatively, if
...u wish to extend your walk, it is
...ssible to continue along the ridge
...visit Lud's Church – a 100m long
...asm traditionally associated with
... Green Chapel in *Sir Gawain and
... Green Knight*.

...To do this, cross the road to reach
...ap in a wall and a sign for a foot-
...h. Go through the gap and walk
...n to reach a gate. Go through this
and continue on a clear path with a
wall to your left.

After half a mile/1km you reach
a signposted junction. Keep straight
on (Danebridge Concession Path). In
a short distance you reach a second
junction. The path to the right (Lud's
Church) provides a short cut (*see*
map), but to complete the circuit
keep straight on (Danebridge), going
through a gate and continuing along
the ridge with a wall now to the right.

When the wall to the right ends
you go through a gate in a fence and
continue along the ridge, eventually
dropping to a wall with a junction on
the near side of it. Go right (Grad-
bach).

A clear path contours around the
hill; through moorland at first, then
into mature mixed woodland. You
reach a signposted junction by a large
tor amongst the trees. Go ahead-right
here (Lud's Church) and you shortly
reach the narrow entrance to Lud's
Church to your right. Walk through
the dark, mossy chasm (it is around
100m long and 20m high), then
continue along the clear path which
emerges from the top.

The path reaches a junction. The
right-hand path is the other end of the
short cut (*see* map). For this route, go
straight on. At the next two junctions, go right (Roach End). From
the second, you start to climb back up
the hill, with a wall to your left. This
leads you back up to the gap in the
wall where you started.

Return either along the top of The
Roaches or along the public road.

24 **Rudyard Reservoir**

A series of paths and tracks making a circuit of a quiet reservoir.
Length: **5¹/₂ miles/9km**; *Height Climbed: undulating.*

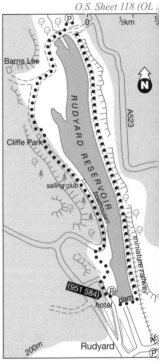

The village of Rudyard – at the south end of the lake – is 2 miles north-west of Leek on the A523/B5331. The main parking is on the edge of the village (turn left after passing under the railway line), but there is a smaller car park by the lake (turn right, into the village, then turn right at the sign for the Activity Centre, just after the hotel). Failing both these, there is a further car park at the north end of the lake (*see* map).

From the car park by the lake, walk back up to the road and turn right. At the first junction keep left (sign for Cliffe Park). When an access road cuts right, keep left again. Navigation on the next section is difficult to describe; fortunately, the junctions are marked by yellow arrows. If you follow these you end up on the road above the lake, behind a row of exotic houses and boathouses.

Beyond the sailing club the road becomes a track and climbs away from the lake. Beyond a gate/stile the track runs through open parkland (watch out for grazing cattle) as it approaches a house (Cliffe Park).

Keep right, walking outside the house grounds, to rejoin a clear vehicle track beyond. When this joins another driveway, keep right, heading back down to the lake.

The track winds round the head of the lake and crosses a bridge. Keep

left beyond this (yellow arrow) to reach the car park.

Turn right immediately, passing under a bridge, to join the clear track running down the east side of the lake. Follow this to the end of the lake and cross the dam to return to the start.